I0151437

O to Be a Dragon

poems by

Sara Sutter

Finishing Line Press
Georgetown, Kentucky

O to Be a Dragon

ACKNOWLEDGMENTS

I am grateful to my teachers, Michele Glazer and John Beer. Thank you to the
editors of the following magazines, in which versions of these poems originally
appeared: *The Awl, elimae, Fence,* and *Lablit.*

Publisher: Leah Maines

Editor: Christen Kincaid

Cover Art: Kristin Fialka

Cover Design: Elizabeth Maines

Printed in the USA on acid-free paper.
Order online: www.finishinglinepress.com
also available on amazon.com

Author inquiries and mail orders:
Finishing Line Press
P. O. Box 1626
Georgetown, Kentucky 40324
U. S. A.

Table of Contents

The Turkey Vulture...1

The Shrew..4

Oestrus Lecture...5

Bed Bugs..10

The Spotted Hyena......................................12

The Changing Snow Chicken....................17

Hagfish..18

Japanning..20

The Sea Cow and The Siren.....................21

A Jellyfish..27

SMOUND...28

To Marianne Moore

The Turkey Vulture

is a gregarious bird
who scavenges
by smell of carcass gasses.

Adapted to suit
a messy diet, her red head
and neck are bare except
thin down covering.

Her primary defense is
vomiting in the eyes
of predators approaching
her half-digested meat nest—

accustomed to gorging herself
if food arises,
such defense releases
weight the vulture flies without.

The regurgitant may be fresh
or foul-smelling, not to disgust—
a human reaction—but
to feed the attacker, another scavenger.

Urohydrosis,
she urinates onto her legs
for antibacterial
and cooling purposes.

A model of resourcefulness,
she "lacks" a syrinx,
or vocal organ,
low hisses when threatened,

grunts for hunger or courting.
Regurgitating urges,
"fragile graces," feared,
yet fearful themselves.

Though where fear resides
courage festers, 'til it bears
its bald, red head. When I
first saw the turkey vulture's

great wingspan
from her small body
in horaltic pose like Moore herself,
black cape and all,

how could I know which words
to assign that bird's heroic form?
Did Moore, too, come night,
cool herself among her own

cold-blooded jewels?
Not woman necessarily,
taloning her chin-up bar,
nesting with her mother,

their apartment filled with art.
Her verse, she said,
"could only be called poetry
because there was no other category

in which to put it." Her leaps and acid,
her Old World—
And so I scavenge
volumes of dead, the extravagant dead,

pick the scraps
with my chicken feet,
"too weak to grasp or lift,"
for the perfect muscle morsel

lump spit. "The imagination
is incapable of creating novelties."
One hopes the flesh
bears juice, juices.

The Shrew

Astute, she always knows
answers regarding displacement
of supposed masters,
       the dumping of night soil,
       specters, floods, or the presence
of a cat or a dog. "Fiercely

territorial." "So
clever he wants to escape." Digs
burrows, echolocates
       via multiharmonic,
       ultrasonic squeaks. "Someone
yelling to the heavens."

They feel each other from
overall-reverb-calls, but just
because he hears, doesn't
       mean he listens. "Better lone-
       ly than unhappy, echo-
loco." "This time," she says to her-

self, "I will make an end
of her once and for all." Concocts
a poison comb, scours
       herself beautiful, and roams
       the hills calling out "I shall
like to be personal!"

Oestrus Lecture

1.

Shall we try and map it?

If so, begin with Proestrus—*pro*, Greek, means
before—when follicles of ovary begin to grow.
Precious pre-fledgling, number-specific for each species,
the lining in the uterus, think crib, gains thickness...

at which width the female, sexually receptive,
"in heat," regulated by gonadotropic hormones,
exhibits sexually receptive behavior—
perhaps signaled "by visible physiologic changes,"

such as elevation of hindquarters. "In few species
labia are reddened, and some may experience
bleeding." Throughout Metestrus and Diestrus, but in the
absence of pregnancy, the uterine lining folds

into itself, a perfect napkin, to be applied
to the next cycle. And for some lucky bitches, there is
a period of rest: anestrus, a seasonal
event conducted by light, an orchestration of glands.
          See: mammalian placental, irrational drives, gadfly.

2.

Rabbits do not have a cycle. They can conceive at almost any moment.

3.

Take Brenda, for example.
Brenda often found herself screaming at her teenage
children during Metestrus. She felt depressed,
angry, hostile, and iso-
lated herself. Sleeping became difficult and dish-
es broke. Poor Brenda bloated, endured breasts that
felt battered, headaches, etc.

Joan also. A thirty-year-
old single woman who grew increasingly restless,
sad, and lethargic at ovulation. Im-
patient, fatter, highly o-
verreactive, eventually suicidal.
Joan believed she was "in the clutches of
a bad mood that would not go."

4.

When they menstruated, they left a trail behind them—"tampons,
pads, rags, sponges, grass, and other absorbent mater-
ials probably for thousands of years." Of women

who fought in the American Civil War, most couldn't
write, not that literate women would record their flow.
Always considered how "open" menstruation, as op-
posed to "closed," influenced men, necessitated conceal-

ment of both blood and odors before participation in—
"but many bled into their clothing, especially
those from rural and lower classes." American lass-
es, migrating westward, animals in clothing also:

Norweigan knitted pads, Italian washables—"for one
wife of the Prophet who had extra blood (non-menstrual)
placed a tray to catch and hold it while she prayed." "The woman
who has a prolonged flow surely must wash herself each

day, and when her period is over, take a woolen
cloth greased with fat or oil (to tie over the privates)"—and in India
women did not bleed at all.

See: Brenda, Joan, Rats, Ewe, Sow.

5.

"Ideally, defloration occurred on her wedding night"
with completion of the first oestrous.

"Artemis tied the ritual knot the husband only un-
tied as he undressed the saffron-veiled
female, who

often used her girdle for noose." "She removed herself."

Notes:

an-especially-creative-time-for-some-women,Red-Flag,blood-
fairy, obstreperous-clot, drybrown-dragon-on-ply, illuminated-
manuscript, vest-of-pad-and-tampon-vestige, o.b.-bullet,
bronze-o.b., Pay-As-You-Flow-Flow-Chart, tea-stained-cotton-
canvas-thread-and-seed-beaded-uterine-network, "The-Goddess"-
while-the-blood-is-still-wet-just-diagnosed-with-a-double-uterus,
red-acrylic-self-portrait-in-the-crotch-of-feminine-undies, toilet-
bowl-overflowing-with-roses, tampax-mice, 10-Tablespoons-A-Month,
Menstrual-Spoor, crimson-copper-clotted blithe-swathe, Step-2-Insert-
Screen-Print, Looking-For-Aunt-Martha-After-The-Afterbirth, red-
nest-pinhole-chocolate-satin, Venus-Sits-Down

Bed Bugs

In early stages, the pests tend to congregate,
mostly in sleeping areas. Fecal-dark and mattress-ridge-enmeshed,
infestations grow and spread
into tufts, skirts, crev-
ices, wall-to-wall-carpet-edges, phones, clocks, smoke-detectors,
televisions,
recessed screws, "grottoes from which issue penetrating draughts which
make you wonder

why you came." [citation needed] Wall louse,
mahogany flat, crimson-rambler,
lone dragoon, chinche, redcoat, *Cimex lectularius*[9]—
ubiquitous presence instilling "panopticonesque-fear." Paired, yet
you may see one bug: "I should like to
be alone." "I should like to

be alone." A stray egg. Nymphs look like adults who can wait 550
days
for food. Engorgement takes 3-10 minutes, but seldom will one know
she's
being bitten. [non-primary source needed] "Then just aft-
er feeding, they crawl away and hide
wherever they hide to digest their meal. Bites may
not lead to serious disease, but to symptoms the bitten exper-

ience chronically: "This bug, this no-
mad who has 'proposed to
land on my hand for life.'" He reproduces solely by
traumatic or hy-
perdermic insemination—when his needle-y-penis injects
her gut "with the concentric
crushing rigor of a python,"

eliminates courtship time and allows for man-
y mates; tears in fabric, ovipositioned, out as well as in. [8][98] "Dis-
regarding secondhand articles
—though the process can be
quite costly—may help." [citation needed] To prevent, take precautions. "It makes
great sense
to avoid
them in the first place." Part the cushions and keep an eye skinned. The
bed bug's

clear-head-incandescent-quality, often mistaken
for a tick, is easy to miss on a scissor tip.

The Spotted Hyena

1.

possesses by far the largest clitoris in the animal kingdom.
Vulva-fused, it's a mysterious clump
"that erects voluntarily," and subordinates lick. Thus,
"her clit will be licked by all other females, males (which are in-
ferior) or cubs."

Similarly endowed species include: squirrel monkey, lemur, bearcat, and
zedonk,
but no one knows the exact name
for her huge clit—her pseudo-penis? clenis?
            Slot, slope, spandrel?

                    Der Kitzler—the tickler, "clitoridis" as in "clitoridis." As
the river
in spring laps the brink of its banks, and the bridge's metal joints widen in
summer heat,

"would it be too bold to imagine in the great length of time all warm-
blooded beings
            arose from one expanding filament?" Yet it may be

partially or totally removed during female circumcision, because Erasmus
Darwin's pro-posed mechanism lay in usefulness of character, in function
————"the clit is not,

2.

however, *functional*"—

—"as if it were
inconceivably arcane,
as symmetrically frigid
as if carved out of chrysoprase
or marble—strict

      with tension, malignant in its
           power over us and deeper than the sea
      when it proffers flattery." Bio-
           logy's cornice, the clit is a consequence,
      an architectural byproduct of
      mounting domes on rounded arches
           of Gothic churches, snails' brooding chambers,
      shoulder hubs of the Irish deer, and

      human mentality. "Any
           diversity resulting from this wall will
      be perceived as too complex, not
           pretty." "Is the clitoris actually
      a dead penis? What is it then?" The clit
           is discovered, rediscovered,
      through empirical documents of male scho-
           lars repeatedly through centuries—

"my brother wants to know."

3.

The full extent of the clitoris was alluded to by Masters and Johnson, but in such a muddled fashion their description vanished. The Federation of Feminism continued this process with a live examination, yet the most commonly consulted cliterary guide is Hippocrates' Urban Dictionary:

> **Clit.** The term Jill uses to refer to her husband's useless tiny cock. "His clit creates no panty bulge, and is never confused with a male penis."
>
> **Clist.** A clit with a cyst, a clit resembling a cyst, or just an abnormally large clit. "The day my girlfriend told me that her clit was actually more than a little bump."
>
> **Boy-clit**. A ridiculously small penis. "Nice boy-clit."
>
> **Huge clit.** A big, hard clitoris that only some women have. These organs can measure up to 3 inches in length and 4 inches in circumference. Huge clits have shafts and knobs and are covered by hoods. "She pulls out the knob of her huge clit, and I engulf it in my mouth."
>
> **Gorilla Mask**. After a lovely evening at Olive Garden (Red Lobster can be substituted if the wait is too long) politely ask your partner to participate in intercourse. Prior to ejaculation position the face directly in front of your organ, and release your seed. Upon completion, reach down with your dominant hand, grab a handful of your partner's pubes, and throw them on his/her/its face. At this point, run to a public place so all can see the gorilla chasing you. "Yeah, they have unlimited breadsticks and salad."

4.

Mermaid babies are born live (as opposed to hatched from eggs). A clitoris (the same color as the tail) is below the urogenital opening, followed by an anus. Mermaid vaginas are slightly smaller than human ones (since male mermaid penises are smaller, explained below), so they tend to be more sexually satisfying to human males. Males have a penis almost as small as a female clitoris the same color as the tail hardly visible (the only plausible explanation to why no one has ever seen a penis on male mermaids). Testes are inside the tail, as opposed to the pelvis, since they require a slightly lower temperature to function properly (the human part is warm-blooded, the tail is cold-blooded). The anus is above the penis.

5.

O tension rod,
nature's rubik's cube,
seat of woman's delight,
hyperlink and genital tubercle—

There is no identifiable correlation
between size and a woman's
"pencil-top eraser."

"The panda develops a false thumb,
                    from the bone of the wrist
                              vis-à-vis the bone of the foot,"

but sexual pleasure might not arise directly from coital efforts. Copulation
is a relatively short affair, at night, with no other hyenas present. "She is
promiscuous, and no enduring

pair-bonds form." Favors young mates or those who join her natal clan.
"Even if he outweighs her, he knows to approach submissively, the more
submissive the better, and if

she chooses to retract her huge clitoris, he may slide beneath to enter."

The Changing Snow Chicken

A type of grouse. A game bird whose
name originates from imitation

of all the grumbling he does—"his
song is more like a croak." Thus few souls go

within earshot. The Changing Snow
Chicken lives in the Arctic, and changes

"from brown in summer to a nice
winter plumage in winter." "Naturally,"

he explains, "this helps me blend in-
to my environment, which I refuse

to leave although it's the harshest
tundra on the planet." This, he tells you

while wagging his comb—his sole
ornament, big as a half-closed fist—

Hagfish

"The most disgusting animal to inhabit the sea."
A hard-brained, horn-toothed, barbelled, pink in-
        vertebrate who emits slime jets from a slime

      battery that runs the length of her body. Vermiform,
wormy. "She ties herself in an o-
        verhand knot to scrape away the glutinous,

   loosening goo that aids her escape from a predator's
hold." "She hates to be held, because
      then she loves it, and then she hates to wait to

       be held." Time "passes," and you, too, slime to fill
       the shape you once hoped to hold. Find yourself
       in an ex-boyfriend's bed—"Okay, go ahead."

   "In captivity, hagfish use the overhand-knot be-
havior 'in reverse' (tail-to-head) to
      assist in pulling hunks of flesh from which-

       ever carcass they hope to enter." A necromancer's
      romance. You roll your car down the hill,
       not when he noted your purple eye shadow,

   dream of being stabbed in the face. "In neuroscience, OLD
HAG ATTACK refers to a threshold
      consciousness of paralysis and hallu-

     cination. When excessive, some consider this culture."
Cry yourself puffy, languid.
      Other days squeeze into yoga poses, skin-

   ny jeans, cocktail stupors. You, a stock character hag who,
"in fairy tales shares traits with the crone."
     As though you need to feel close to death to know

"you are what you're waiting for." "If we admit to the existence of the unconscious, we search
for something within ourselves to find and be

disgusted by." Wake. See how yellow your teeth are growing.

Japanning

Evaporated sap deposited
in insects made perfect cabinet laminae. "Flakes
from the carcass melted to a thin varnish,"
a resin-based insoluble shellac varnish
yielding hard-polished glossy surfaces,
"decoration layers," overlaying
a black base. Anterior scenes could be
> scrolled with foliage, trellis panels,
> pagodas, branch-perched parrots,
> a boar and hound hunt vignette,
> or, more commonly, a cluster
> of newborn Nubians. Today's
specimen, however, bear scatters
of cracks and gossamer losses,
"kidney-shaped chips in the coats and boxes'
interior gilt nicked away." Damage becomes
authenticity's measure. Collectors seek tangible
attrition: "He would rattle off inventory
> in his sleep. He was
> such a brain." "Your blood
> relies on four special valves
> inside the heart." "The enlightened psyche
> accepts that death
> is part of love." "Et cetera."

The Sea Cow and the Siren

1.

     Sea cows use forelimbs for paddling.
     They also move without
trying, gliding on buried currents

to protected areas—
        mangroves—where they keep their snout down-
        turned to sniff the seagrasses,
and avoid the long black eyes of boats

that cut the water. She ne-
        ver leaves it, but even havens
        hold dangers. Males, for instance,
"establish territory

to lure bleeding females to
        watch trespassers be created
        then vanquished"—a process known
as lekking. One imagines

that with Jane Austen's sitting-room graces the sea cow smiles
through her boredom, that boredom is zoonotic, "transmitted
between species," as in males attempting to mate
with the same female inflicting injury to her and each other.

                             She
copulates with many who swim up but not all—"me?" "no." "me?"
"no."—mounting from below, thus increasing chances of death
and conception.

2.

Hunted widely, she became
        legend—a tale of remnant

hind limb bones in a tail of scales; a "she
        who sings to seamen throws them off, asking

                for it," a "she who knows
                both past and future," a "she whose song

        takes effect midday
    in windless puddles":

Magdalena T. de la Riva, who appeared in almost 80
films, was on her way home from the broadcasting
studio when a Pontiac cut

her way, and a gang forcibly took her at Swanky Hotel. She was
left at the Free Press Building near Channel 5.
Another spotlit rape case became

so popular, achieving political and international
significance for the Visiting Forces A-
greement: Suzette alleged she was

by four U.S. Marines. A few days later, she changed her
statements and name. One man
was selected, and Nicole re-
ceived the chance to go to the U.S.

3.

According to a report, the victim, an only daughter of a
prominent family, was riding on a motorcycle with her boyfriend
along a road in a village when a group of men hit them with a
wooden club. The boy lost consciousness, and the men brought
the girl to an area near the police headquarters. The men took
turns raping the girl. While they were brutalizing her, her cell
phone rang. The girl's mother was on the line asking about her
daughter's whereabouts. The man who answered the phone told
the mother that her daughter was fornicating. He said it in a
most vulgar way in the local dialect, and I don't want to quote
what he said. The girl was found the following day. She looked
like she had been clubbed. Her body bore marks of beating. Her
sexual organ was slashed and stuffed with sand, plastic and pieces
of wood. The victim— "Janet," not her real name—claimed, in
a dying declaration, that she was gang-raped repeatedly by four
men, one of whom she named. The father told reporters that
they were not aware of her ordeal until shortly before she died,
when they noticed unusual things about her. Police have jointly
captured two of the gang. Remnants on the scene include: one 38
revolver snubnose with 4 live ammunition, 1 white container, 3
cellular phones, and a pearl (earring).

4.

Love is a battlefield. For weaponry, they used de-
lineation. Various gray
human daubs on one Great Northern Expedition.

Blank areas on maps reddened. Tanks of tissue docked in
Russia—they parsed her parts: a
cool bionic arm, azure hues, axilla left breast left

buttock left calf left chest left colon left coronary
artery left where "a great
sinner lyeth here," and, "dorsal fins are for pussies." These

acts produced the hand in the sea cow.

5.

She folds her arms across her chest
        to medially rotate the scapulae
                while bending the trunk. Crepitates.
                        Becomes a box

that consists of small boxes, glass
        slides, blood collection devices, nail picks, swabs,
                plastic bags of clothing fibers, hair,
                        saliva, se-

men and other fluid, docu-
        mentation forms and labels which may provide
                evidence for prosecution in
                        a criminal

trial—but backlog may persist
        until everyone involved is dead.

6.

If the victim lives to see her test
results processed, "50-60% prove
positive for (biological) mater-
ial that does not belong to her." The source may be

identified by a facial
recognition system, voice recording,
gait analysis or from the content of
his writing—"typical phrases, factual bias,

misspellings." In the Siren's case:

"she has the body of a bird with only the head or upper body of a woman
or just bird legs."

These characteristics helped the seamen
discern her form before hearing her song.
They had time to block their ears with wax, and

escape.

A Jellyfish

Visible, visible,
not-even-vertebrate,
multiorgan misnomer
of multiple morphologies. "Large groups swarm small spaces,

implying an ability
to stay together." Another
collective name is smack—
a kiss, a hit, a precision.
Jellies sessile, sans
peduncle, parasitic. A

passive hunter using
tentacles for drift nets
should fish brush its unobserved
delicate tissue protectors.
Distraught meaninglessness

of needing to feed, ingest through
one mid-bell-hole. "To constitute
identity is to
exist precisely." Nevermind
your fluctuating charm,
your bloomy nature; polypoid

+ egg + sperm =
larval form planula.
Measured in millimeters,
"what is your planula?" Dawn, spawn,
abandon your intent.

SMOUND

*Scents, like sounds, appear to influence the olfactory nerve in
certain definite degrees.*   —Scientific American

Cup of coffee thrice-sized the anesthetized mice
  gave a start, a SMOUND,
    to the laboratory table
      one afternoon. Union newfound,

a portmanteau, mot-valise, of smell and sound—SMOUND—
  the urge to pack one word
    inside another: beefalo, zee-
      donk. "A potent olfactory

gustatory implication," Wesson observed
  tuberculate spikes.
    "He picked his mug back up. Sip. Clunk. Spike."
      Japanoise. "He SMOUNDED it!" "What

your brain does is take objects and SMOUNDS them into
  one great sensory
    energy." Thus a toe pinch might soothe
      bad moods, calf rub quell intellect.

Existence of SMOUND sense has broad implications:
  saffron risotto
    paired with Beyoncé in lieu of
      Beethoven; buckets-o-chicken

eaten by SMOUNDING the smog they're cooked in.
  Listen to cumin.
    Smell the cello's octave of odor.
      "The systematic derangement

of the senses is means to perceive awareness"—one
  brutal sense onslaught
    before the great void takes over, when
      the mouse body is no longer

separate from its environment; "unspeakab-
le torment, where he
needs superhuman strength, where he be-
comes the great invalid, the great
criminal, accursed, the Supreme Scientist!"
Sip. Clunk. Spike.
Repetition is sy-
nonymous with accuracy.

"Long, immense, intimidating, rational de-
rangement." Love. Suffer-
ing. Smadness;

Observations:

anesthetized mice anesthetized mice anesthetized mice
anesthetized mice anesthetized mice anesthetized mice
anesthetized mice anesthetized mice anesthetized mice
anesthetized mice anesthetized miSMOUNDce anesthetized
mSMOUNDice anesthetized mice anesthetized mice anesthetized
micSMOUNDe anesthetized mice
anesthetized mice anesthetized mice anesthetized mice
anesthetized mice anesthetized SMOUNDSMOUNDmice
anesthetized mice anesthetized mice anesthetized mice
anesthetized mice anesthetized mice anesthetizSMOUNDed mice
anesthetized mice
anesthetized mice anesthetized mice anesthetized mice
anesthetized mice anesthetized mice anesthetized mice
anesthetized mice anesthetized mice anesthetized mice
anesthetized mice anesthetized miceSMOUND anesthetized mice
anesthetized mice

29

Sara Sutter is a writer and professor living in Portland, Oregon. Support for her work has come from Sou'wester Lodge in Washington and Gullkistan Center for Creative People in Iceland. Sara also authored *Sirenomelia* (Poor Claudia 2013).